Copyrighted mater

Guidelines on how to play
CORNET

Bonus songs

Eleanor Kensington

Copyright © 2024 by Eleanor Kensington

All rights reserved. No part of this publication may be reproduced, distributed, or transmitted in any form or by any means, including photocopying, recording, or other electronic or mechanical methods, without the prior written permission of the publisher, except in the case of brief quotations embodied in critical reviews and certain other noncommercial uses permitted by copyright law.

Table of Contents

Chapter 1 10

Getting Started 10

    Introduction to the Cornet 10

Chapter 2 16

Posture and Breathing 16

    Proper Posture While Playing 16

Chapter 3 28

Embouchure and Mouthpiece 28

Chapter 4 39

Basic Techniques 39

Chapter 5 52

Music Theory Basics 52

    Introduction to Music Notation 52

Chapter 6 64

Beginning Repertoire 64

    Easy Songs and Melodies to Practice 64

Chapter 7 76

Developing Skills 76

    Intermediate Techniques for Advancing Players 76

Chapter 8 90

Cornet Maintenance 90

Chapter 9 104

Playing with Others 104

Chapter 10 119

Cornet in Different Musical Genres..119

Chapter 11 133

Performance Tips 133

Chapter 12 150

Conclusion...150

Bonus 158

Introduction

The cornet holds a rich history and profound significance in the realm of brass instruments. Originating in the early 19th century, the cornet evolved from its predecessors, such as the post horn and the keyed bugle, to become a staple in various musical genres. Developed alongside the rise of brass bands and military ensembles, the cornet quickly gained popularity due to its clear, mellow tone and versatility in both solo and ensemble settings.

Throughout its history, the cornet has played a vital role in shaping musical compositions and performances. Its distinct sound has been featured prominently in orchestral works, brass band arrangements, jazz improvisations, and even popular music genres. Renowned composers and virtuoso performers have showcased the cornet's expressive capabilities, contributing to its enduring legacy in the world of music.

In this comprehensive guide, we will delve into the fundamentals of playing the cornet, from mastering basic techniques to exploring advanced repertoire. Whether you're a beginner seeking to embark on your musical journey or an experienced musician looking to refine your skills, this book aims to provide you with the knowledge and resources needed to excel on this remarkable instrument.

Throughout the chapters of this book, we will cover everything you need to know to become proficient in playing the cornet. From understanding the basic components of the instrument to mastering advanced techniques, each section is carefully crafted to provide you with clear and concise instructions.

An overview of what this book will cover:

1. Getting Started: We'll begin by introducing you to the cornet, its parts, and how to assemble and care for your instrument.

2. Posture and Breathing: Learn the importance of proper posture and breathing techniques for playing the cornet effectively.

3. Embouchure and Mouthpiece: Discover how to form a correct embouchure and select the right mouthpiece for your playing style.

4. Basic Techniques: Master the foundational techniques of holding the cornet, producing sound, and playing simple notes and scales.

5. Music Theory Basics: Gain a fundamental understanding of music notation, rhythms, and reading notes on the staff.

6. Beginning Repertoire: Start playing music with easy songs and melodies designed for beginners.

7. Developing Skills: Progress to intermediate techniques, exercises, and more complex musical pieces to enhance your skills.

8. Cornet Maintenance: Learn how to clean, care for, and troubleshoot common issues with your instrument.

9. Playing with Others: Explore the dynamics of playing in groups, from brass ensembles to bands, and develop essential ensemble skills.

10. Cornet in Different Musical Genres: Discover the versatility of the cornet and its role in various musical genres, including jazz, classical, and more.

11. Performance Tips: Get valuable advice on overcoming stage fright, preparing for auditions, and delivering polished performances.

12. Conclusion: Wrap up your journey with a recap of key points and encouragement to continue your musical exploration.

Whether you're dreaming of performing on stage or simply seeking a fulfilling hobby, this book is your comprehensive guide to unlocking the beauty and potential of the cornet. Let's embark on this musical journey together!

Chapter 1

Getting Started

Introduction to the Cornet

Welcome to Chapter 1 of "Learn to Play the Cornet: A Comprehensive Guide for Beginners." In this chapter, we will introduce you to the cornet, a fascinating and versatile brass instrument with a rich history and unique sound.

The cornet is a member of the brass family, similar in appearance to the trumpet but with some distinct differences. It features a conical bore, which gives it a mellower and more rounded tone compared to the brighter sound of the trumpet. The cornet also typically has a more compact and slightly curved shape, making it easier to hold and play for extended periods.

Originally developed in the early 19th century, the cornet quickly gained popularity in various musical settings, including military bands, brass bands, orchestras, and jazz ensembles. Its expressive tone and agile playing characteristics have made it a favorite among composers and performers alike, with a repertoire spanning classical, jazz, and popular music genres.

One of the defining features of the cornet is its ability to blend seamlessly with other instruments, making it an essential component of ensemble playing. Whether you're playing in a brass band, orchestra, or small ensemble, the cornet's versatile sound can adapt to a wide range of musical styles and settings.

Throughout this chapter, we will explore the basic components of the cornet, including its various parts and how to assemble them properly. By the end of this chapter, you will have a solid understanding of the instrument itself, laying the foundation for your journey to becoming a proficient cornet player. Let's dive in and explore the world of the cornet together!

How to Assemble and Care for Your Instrument

Now that you're familiar with the parts of the cornet, let's discuss how to assemble and care for your instrument properly. Proper assembly and maintenance are crucial for keeping your cornet in optimal playing condition and ensuring its longevity.

1. Assembling Your Cornet:

   - Start by laying out all the parts of your cornet in front of you, including the main body, valves, valve slides, mouthpiece, and any accessories.

   - Carefully insert the mouthpiece into the mouthpiece receiver, ensuring a snug fit without forcing it.

- Align the valve guides on the valves with their respective valve casings on the cornet.

- Gently insert each valve into its casing, taking care not to damage the valve or casing.

- Once all the valves are in place, press down on each valve firmly to ensure they are seated correctly.

- Attach any valve slides by aligning them with their respective valve casings and sliding them into place.

2. Caring for Your Cornet:

- After each playing session, disassemble your cornet and wipe down the exterior with a clean, soft cloth to remove any moisture or fingerprints.

- Use a valve casing brush to clean inside the valve casings and remove any debris or buildup.

- Inspect the valve pistons regularly for signs of wear or damage. If necessary, lubricate the valves with valve oil to ensure smooth operation.

- Clean the mouthpiece regularly with warm, soapy water and a mouthpiece brush to remove any residue or bacteria.

- Check the alignment of the valve slides and main tuning slide regularly to ensure they move freely without sticking.

- Store your cornet in a sturdy case when not in use to protect it from dust, humidity, and accidental damage.

By following these steps, you can keep your cornet in excellent playing condition and ensure it continues to produce beautiful music for years to come. In the next chapter, we'll discuss the importance of proper posture and breathing techniques for playing the cornet effectively. Let's continue our journey of learning and exploration together!

Chapter 2

Posture and Breathing

Proper Posture While Playing

Achieving proper posture is essential for playing the cornet effectively and avoiding discomfort or injury. Proper posture allows for optimal breath control, instrument handling, and overall performance. Here's a detailed guide on achieving and maintaining correct posture while playing the cornet:

1. Seated Posture:

   - Sit on a straight-backed chair with your feet flat on the floor and your back upright.

   - Keep your shoulders relaxed and your chest comfortably lifted.

- Position the cornet in front of you, with the bell facing slightly upward and the leadpipe angled toward your mouth.

2. Standing Posture:

  - Stand with your feet shoulder-width apart and your weight evenly distributed between both legs.

  - Keep your knees slightly bent to maintain balance and flexibility.

  - Stand tall with your spine straight and your shoulders relaxed.

  - Hold the cornet with your left hand supporting the instrument's weight and your right hand on the valves.

3. Hand and Arm Position:

  - Position your left hand comfortably under the leadpipe, with your fingers curved and resting lightly on the valve casing.

- Keep your right hand relaxed and close to your body, with your fingers poised over the valve buttons.

- Avoid tensing your hands or gripping the cornet too tightly, as this can restrict blood flow and impede dexterity.

4. Head and Neck Position:

- Keep your head level and balanced over your spine, avoiding excessive tilting or turning.

- Position your chin parallel to the ground, with your jaw relaxed and slightly forward.

- Avoid straining your neck or craning your head forward to reach the mouthpiece.

5. Breathing Posture:

- Take deep, diaphragmatic breaths by expanding your abdomen as you inhale.

- Keep your chest lifted and your shoulders relaxed to allow for unrestricted airflow.

- Maintain a tall, open posture to maximize lung capacity and breath support.

6. Mirror Check:

- Use a mirror to check your posture regularly while practicing.

- Pay attention to any tension or slouching and make adjustments as needed to maintain proper alignment.

By practicing proper posture consistently, you'll develop a strong foundation for playing the cornet with ease and confidence. In the next section, we'll explore techniques for effective breathing to further enhance your playing ability. Let's continue refining our skills and mastering the art of cornet playing together!

The importance of breathing techniques cannot be overstated when it comes to playing the cornet. Proper breathing is fundamental to producing a beautiful tone, maintaining control over dynamics, and executing musical phrases with precision and expression. Here's why mastering breathing techniques is crucial for cornet players:

1. Tone Production: Effective breathing is essential for producing a rich, resonant tone on the cornet. By taking deep breaths and engaging the diaphragm, players can achieve optimal air support, resulting in a full-bodied sound with clarity and projection.

2. Controlled Dynamics: Proper breathing allows cornet players to control the volume and intensity of their playing. By regulating the flow of air and adjusting the breath pressure, musicians can

seamlessly transition between soft, gentle passages and powerful, dynamic passages.

3. Sustained Phrasing: Good breathing techniques enable cornet players to sustain musical phrases with consistency and continuity. By maintaining a steady flow of air and pacing their breaths effectively, musicians can play longer phrases without interruption, enhancing the overall musical expression and coherence.

4. Extended Endurance: Developing strong breathing muscles and efficient breath management techniques can significantly improve a cornet player's endurance. With proper breathing, musicians can sustain their playing for longer periods without experiencing fatigue or breathlessness, allowing for extended practice sessions and performances.

5. Artistic Expression: Breath control is essential for conveying emotion and expression in music. By mastering breathing techniques, cornet players can shape their phrases with nuance, sensitivity, and musicality, bringing out the subtleties and nuances of the music they perform.

6. Physical Relaxation: Conscious breathing promotes relaxation and reduces tension in the body, enabling cornet players to play with greater ease and fluidity. By focusing on deep, controlled breaths, musicians can alleviate physical strain and maintain a relaxed posture, minimizing the risk of muscle fatigue and injury.

In essence, mastering breathing techniques is paramount for achieving technical proficiency, musicality, and artistic expression on the cornet. Through dedicated practice and attention to breath control, cornet players can unlock their full potential and elevate their playing to new heights.

Improving breathing control is essential for cornet players to enhance their performance and musical expression. Here are some exercises specifically designed to develop breath control and efficiency:

1. Diaphragmatic Breathing:

  - Lie down on your back or sit comfortably with your back straight.

  - Place one hand on your abdomen and the other on your chest.

  - Inhale deeply through your nose, focusing on expanding your abdomen rather than lifting your chest.

  - Feel your abdomen rise as you inhale, then exhale slowly and steadily through your mouth, allowing your abdomen to fall.

  - Repeat this exercise, focusing on maintaining a steady, controlled breath pattern.

2. Breath Support Exercises:

   - Stand or sit with good posture, and take a deep breath.

   - Exhale forcefully and steadily through your mouth, as if blowing out a candle.

   - Practice sustaining a steady stream of air for as long as possible, maintaining consistent breath pressure throughout the exhale.

   - Repeat this exercise, gradually increasing the duration of each exhale as your breath control improves.

3. Long Tones:

   - Choose a comfortable note on your cornet and play it with a steady, full breath.

   - Sustain the note for as long as possible while maintaining a consistent tone and volume.

- Focus on using your breath support to sustain the note evenly from start to finish, avoiding any fluctuations in pitch or volume.

- Repeat this exercise on different notes, gradually extending the duration of each sustained tone as your breath control improves.

4. Interval Exercises:

- Play a simple sequence of intervals (e.g., ascending or descending scales, arpeggios) on your cornet.

- Focus on maintaining a smooth, controlled airflow between each note, using your breath support to control the dynamics and articulation.

- Pay attention to the transition between notes, ensuring that each note begins and ends cleanly without interruptions or inconsistencies in tone.

5. Dynamic Control Exercises:

- Choose a single note and practice playing it at various dynamic levels (e.g., pianissimo to fortissimo).

- Use your breath control to regulate the volume and intensity of each note, focusing on achieving a smooth and gradual transition between dynamic levels.

- Experiment with crescendos, decrescendos, and sudden dynamic changes, paying attention to how your breath control influences the sound and expression of the music.

Incorporate these breathing exercises into your daily practice routine to develop greater control, stamina, and flexibility in your breathing technique. Consistent practice and mindful attention to breath control will significantly enhance your performance on the cornet and contribute to your overall musicality and expression.

Chapter 3

Embouchure and Mouthpiece
What is Embouchure?

Embouchure refers to the way in which a musician shapes their lips, mouth, and facial muscles to produce sound on a wind instrument like the cornet. It plays a crucial role in determining the quality, tone, and control of the sound produced. Developing a strong and flexible embouchure is essential for achieving mastery and proficiency on the cornet.

The embouchure is formed by the coordination of several facial muscles, including the lips, cheeks, jaw, and tongue. Each of these elements contributes to the overall control and precision of the sound produced. A well-developed embouchure allows the cornet player to produce a wide range of tones, dynamics, and articulations with ease and consistency.

Key aspects of a successful embouchure include:

1. Lip Placement: The lips are the primary source of vibration on the cornet. A proper embouchure involves positioning the lips against the mouthpiece in a way that allows for efficient vibration and resonance. The corners of the mouth should be firm but flexible, with the center of the lips forming a cushion against the mouthpiece rim.

2. Mouthpiece Pressure: The amount of pressure applied to the mouthpiece by the lips affects the pitch, tone, and control of the sound. Too much pressure can constrict the airflow and lead to a pinched or strained sound, while too little pressure can result in a weak or unfocused tone.

Finding the right balance of pressure is essential for achieving a clear and resonant sound.

3. Air Support: The embouchure works in conjunction with proper breath support to control the flow of air through the instrument. By engaging the diaphragm and abdominal muscles, the cornet player can regulate the speed and intensity of the airflow, resulting in greater control over dynamics, articulation, and tone color.

4. Flexibility and Endurance: Developing flexibility and endurance in the embouchure muscles is essential for sustained playing and technical proficiency. Regular practice of embouchure exercises and flexibility drills can help strengthen these muscles and improve their responsiveness and stamina over time.

In summary, the embouchure is the foundation of brass instrument playing, serving as the interface between the player and the instrument. By mastering the principles of embouchure and developing proper technique and control, cornet players can unlock their full potential and achieve excellence in their musical performance.

Forming a correct embouchure is crucial for producing a clear and resonant sound on the cornet. Here's a step-by-step guide to help you develop a proper embouchure:

1. Relaxation: Start by relaxing your facial muscles, jaw, and lips. Tension can hinder your ability to form a flexible and responsive embouchure.

2. Positioning: Hold the cornet with your left hand and bring the mouthpiece to your lips with your right hand. Position the mouthpiece centered on your lips, slightly above the center of your mouth.

3. Lip Placement: Form a firm but relaxed seal with your lips around the mouthpiece. The corners of your mouth should be firm, while the center of your lips should be soft and cushioned against the mouthpiece rim.

4. Centering: Aim to center the mouthpiece on your lips, with equal pressure exerted by both upper and lower lips. Avoid favoring one side or the other, as this can lead to unevenness in tone and intonation.

5. Smile Formation: Create a slight smile shape with your lips, as if saying "eee." This helps to lift the corners of your mouth and provides support for the embouchure.

6. Teeth and Jaw: Keep your teeth slightly apart, with the lower jaw relaxed and slightly forward. Avoid clenching your teeth or biting down on the

mouthpiece, as this can restrict airflow and inhibit flexibility in the embouchure.

7. Airflow: Take a deep breath and focus on directing the airflow through the center of the lips into the mouthpiece. Imagine blowing a steady stream of air through a straw, with consistent pressure and control.

8. Experiment: Once you have a basic embouchure formed, experiment with slight adjustments to find the optimal position for producing a clear and resonant sound. Pay attention to the quality of the sound and how it feels to play with different embouchure variations.

9. Practice: Practice forming and maintaining your embouchure regularly, starting with short practice sessions and gradually increasing the duration as your muscles strengthen and adapt. Incorporate

long tones, scales, and simple melodies into your practice routine to develop control and consistency in your embouchure.

By following these steps and dedicating time to practice and experimentation, you can develop a correct embouchure that will lay the foundation for beautiful and expressive cornet playing. Remember to be patient and persistent, as embouchure development takes time and consistent effort.

Choosing the right mouthpiece is essential for achieving optimal sound, comfort, and playability on the cornet. Here's a guide to help you select the right mouthpiece:

1. **Consider Your Playing Level:** Beginners may benefit from a mouthpiece with a medium-sized cup and a comfortable rim width, as it provides a good balance of support and flexibility. More

advanced players may prefer a mouthpiece with specific features tailored to their playing style and needs.

2. **Understand Mouthpiece Components:**

   - Cup: The depth and shape of the cup affect the tone and response of the cornet. Shallower cups produce brighter sounds and facilitate higher notes, while deeper cups produce warmer, darker tones and offer greater control in the lower register.

   - Rim: The width, contour, and inner bite of the rim influence comfort and endurance. A wider rim provides more support and stability, while a narrower rim allows for greater flexibility and agility.

   - Throat: The throat diameter determines the airflow and resistance of the mouthpiece. A larger throat diameter results in a freer, more open feel, while a smaller throat diameter offers greater resistance and control.

- Backbore: The backbore shape and size affect the projection and balance of the sound. A tighter backbore produces a focused, compact sound, while a more open backbore yields a broader, fuller sound.

3. **Consult with a Teacher or Professional**: Seek guidance from a qualified instructor or experienced cornet player who can assess your playing style, skill level, and individual needs. They can provide valuable insights and recommendations based on their expertise and knowledge.

4. **Try Different Mouthpieces**: Experiment with different mouthpieces to find the one that best suits your preferences and playing requirements. Visit a music store with a wide selection of

mouthpieces, and try several options to compare their sound, feel, and response.

5. **Consider the Musical Context:** Take into account the musical genres and settings in which you'll be playing the cornet. Different mouthpiece designs may be more suitable for classical, jazz, or marching band repertoire, so choose one that complements your musical goals and performance requirements.

6. **Seek Feedback:** Once you've narrowed down your options, seek feedback from your teacher, fellow musicians, or trusted advisors. They can offer valuable insights and perspectives to help you make an informed decision.

Remember that finding the right mouthpiece may require some experimentation and adjustment. Be open to trying different options and refining your choice based on your playing experience and feedback from others. Ultimately, the goal is to find a mouthpiece that enhances your sound, comfort, and enjoyment of playing the cornet.

Chapter 4

Basic Techniques
Holding the Cornet Correctly

Properly holding the cornet is fundamental for developing good playing habits, achieving comfort, and maximizing control over the instrument. Here's a step-by-step guide to holding the cornet correctly:

1. Seated Position:

   - Sit on a chair with a straight back and your feet flat on the floor.

   - Keep your back upright and your shoulders relaxed to allow for easy movement and breathing.

2. Standing Position:

- Stand tall with your feet shoulder-width apart and your weight evenly distributed between both legs.

- Maintain good posture with your spine straight and your shoulders relaxed.

3. Left Hand Position:

- Hold the cornet with your left hand, placing your thumb through the loop on the leadpipe.

- Position your index, middle, and ring fingers on the valve casing, with your pinky finger resting on the pinky ring or brace (if your cornet has one).

- Keep your fingers curved and relaxed, hovering over the valve buttons for easy access.

4. Right Hand Position:

- Place your right hand on the valves, with your thumb resting on the side of the valve casing opposite your left thumb.

- Position your index, middle, and ring fingers on the valve buttons, with your pinky finger resting on the side of the valve casing for support.

- Maintain a relaxed grip on the valves, avoiding excessive tension or pressure.

5. Balancing the Cornet:

- Hold the cornet at a slight angle, with the bell facing slightly upward and the leadpipe angled toward your mouth.

- Keep the instrument balanced and stable, with your left hand providing support and your right hand guiding the valves.

6. Alignment:

- Ensure that the leadpipe is centered in front of your face, with the mouthpiece positioned at a comfortable distance from your lips.

- Align the instrument with your body's natural posture, avoiding any twisting or contorting of your torso.

7. Relaxation:

- Maintain a relaxed and natural grip on the cornet, avoiding unnecessary tension or strain in your hands, arms, or shoulders.

- Focus on maintaining a comfortable and balanced posture, allowing for freedom of movement and flexibility while playing.

8. Practice:

- Spend time practicing holding the cornet correctly, both seated and standing.

- Pay attention to any discomfort or tension and make adjustments as needed to ensure comfort and ease of playing.

By mastering the proper technique for holding the cornet, you'll establish a solid foundation for developing your playing skills and achieving success on the instrument. Practice regularly and focus on maintaining good posture, relaxation, and balance to maximize your playing potential.

Producing your first sound on the cornet is an exciting milestone in your musical journey.

1. Mouthpiece Placement:

  - Hold the cornet securely with your left hand, ensuring that it is balanced and stable.

  - Position the mouthpiece at the center of your lips, slightly above the center of your mouth.

2. Embouchure Formation:

  - Form a firm but relaxed seal with your lips around the mouthpiece.

- Create a slight smile shape with your lips, as if saying "eee," to provide support for the embouchure.

3. Breath Control:

   - Take a deep breath and focus on engaging your diaphragm and abdominal muscles.

   - Aim to produce a steady stream of air, maintaining consistent pressure and flow.

4. Initial Buzz:

   - With the mouthpiece in place and your embouchure formed, exhale gently through the mouthpiece.

   - Experiment with different amounts of air pressure and lip tension to find the optimal balance for producing a buzz.

5. Finding the Sound:

- As you exhale through the mouthpiece, focus on creating a buzzing sensation against your lips.

- Gradually increase the airflow and lip tension until you hear a clear, resonant buzz.

6. Transition to the Cornet:

- Once you can produce a consistent buzz on the mouthpiece, try adding the cornet into the equation.

- Bring the cornet to your lips, maintaining the same embouchure and airflow as when buzzing on the mouthpiece.

7. Play a Note:

- With the cornet in position and your embouchure formed, exhale steadily through the instrument.

- Press down one of the valve buttons to change the length of tubing and produce a pitch.

- Start with a simple note, such as the open C or G, and focus on achieving a clear and centered tone.

8. Experimentation and Adjustment:

 - Experiment with different mouthpiece placements, embouchure shapes, and breath pressures to refine your sound.

 - Listen carefully to the tone and quality of your sound, and make adjustments as needed to achieve the desired result.

9. Practice Regularly:

 - Spend time each day practicing producing sound on the cornet, focusing on consistency and control.

 - Gradually expand your range and repertoire as you become more comfortable and confident with your sound production.

Remember, producing your first sound may take some time and patience, so don't be discouraged if it doesn't happen immediately. Keep practicing, stay focused on proper technique, and enjoy the process of making music on the cornet. With dedication and persistence, you'll soon be producing beautiful melodies and enjoying the rewards of your hard work.

Learning to play simple notes and scales is an essential step in mastering the cornet.

1. Understanding Notes:

   - Familiarize yourself with the basic notes of the cornet, which include open notes (no valves pressed) and notes produced by pressing down the valve buttons.

   - Start by learning the names and fingerings for the open notes, typically C, G, and low F.

2. Fingering Chart:

- Refer to a cornet fingering chart to learn the fingerings for each note on the instrument.

- Practice pressing down the valve buttons individually and in combination to produce different pitches.

3. Playing Simple Melodies:

- Choose a simple melody or exercise to practice, such as "Mary Had a Little Lamb" or a beginner-friendly etude.

- Use the fingering chart to identify the notes in the melody and practice playing them one at a time, focusing on accuracy and clarity.

4. Slow Practice:

- Start by playing the melody slowly and deliberately, focusing on hitting each note cleanly and evenly.

- Pay attention to your fingerings, embouchure, and breath control to ensure proper technique.

5. Building Speed and Agility:

  - Once you're comfortable with the melody at a slow tempo, gradually increase the speed to build speed and agility.

  - Practice playing the melody at different tempos, gradually pushing yourself to play faster while maintaining control and accuracy.

6. Playing Scales:

  - Begin by learning simple scales, such as the C major scale or the G major scale.

  - Practice playing each scale slowly and evenly, focusing on playing each note with a consistent tone and articulation.

7. Two-Octave Scales:

- Once you're comfortable with single-octave scales, challenge yourself to play two-octave scales.

 - Practice ascending and descending through the scale smoothly, paying attention to proper fingerings and breath control.

8. Variations and Patterns:

 - Experiment with different variations and patterns within the scales, such as arpeggios, thirds, and chromatic passages.

 - Practice these variations slowly at first, gradually increasing the speed and complexity as you become more proficient.

9. Regular Practice:

 - Dedicate time each day to practicing simple notes and scales on the cornet, focusing on building strength, coordination, and confidence.

- Set specific goals for yourself, such as mastering a particular scale or increasing your speed by a certain amount, and track your progress over time.

By following these steps and practicing regularly, you'll gradually build your skills and confidence on the cornet, laying the foundation for more advanced playing techniques and repertoire. Enjoy the process of learning and exploring the possibilities of the instrument, and don't hesitate to seek guidance from a qualified instructor if you encounter any challenges along the way.

Chapter 5

Music Theory Basics

Introduction to Music Notation

Understanding music notation is essential for learning to play the cornet and interpreting written music. Here's an introduction to music notation to help you get started:

1. Staff: Music notation is written on a set of horizontal lines and spaces called a staff. The staff consists of five lines and four spaces, with each line and space representing a different pitch.

2. Clef: A clef is a symbol placed at the beginning of the staff to indicate the range of pitches and the position of notes on the staff. The most common clef used for cornet music is the treble clef, which positions middle C on the second line of the staff.

3. Notes: Notes are symbols used to represent musical pitches on the staff. Each note is placed on a line or space of the staff, indicating the pitch to be played.

4. Note Durations: Notes also indicate the duration or length of time that a pitch should be played. Different types of notes represent different durations, ranging from whole notes (which last for four beats) to sixteenth notes (which last for a fraction of a beat).

5. Rests: Rests are symbols used to indicate periods of silence in music. Like notes, rests come in different durations, corresponding to the lengths of the notes they represent.

6. Time Signature: The time signature is a symbol placed at the beginning of a piece of music to indicate the number of beats per measure and the type of note that receives one beat. Common time

signatures include 4/4 (four beats per measure, quarter note receives one beat) and 3/4 (three beats per measure, quarter note receives one beat).

7. Key Signature: The key signature is a set of sharps or flats placed at the beginning of a piece of music to indicate the key in which the music is written. Key signatures help determine which notes are sharp or flat throughout the piece.

8. Bar Lines: Bar lines are vertical lines that divide the staff into measures or bars. Each measure contains a specific number of beats as indicated by the time signature.

9. Repeat Signs: Repeat signs are symbols placed at the beginning and end of a section of music to indicate that the section should be repeated.

10. Dynamics: Dynamics are symbols used to indicate the volume or intensity of music.

Common dynamic markings include forte (loud), piano (soft), crescendo (gradually getting louder), and decrescendo (gradually getting softer).

By familiarizing yourself with these basic elements of music notation, you'll be better equipped to read and interpret written music for the cornet. Practice identifying notes, rhythms, and other symbols on the staff, and gradually build your understanding of how they come together to create music.

Understanding rhythms and time signatures is essential for interpreting and playing music accurately on the cornet

1. Rhythm Basics:

   - Rhythm refers to the organization of sounds and silences in music over time.

   - Each note and rest has a specific duration, represented by its shape and position on the staff.

2. Note Durations:

   - Whole Note: Represents four beats (or a whole measure) and is typically an open circle.

   - Half Note: Represents two beats and is an open circle with a stem.

   - Quarter Note: Represents one beat and is a closed circle with a stem.

   - Eighth Note: Represents half a beat and is a closed circle with a stem and one flag.

   - Sixteenth Note: Represents a quarter of a beat and is a closed circle with a stem and two flags.

3. Rest Durations:

   - Whole Rest: Indicates four beats of silence and is represented by a rectangle hanging from the fourth line of the staff.

- Half Rest: Indicates two beats of silence and is represented by a rectangle sitting on top of the third line of the staff.

- Quarter Rest: Indicates one beat of silence and looks like a squiggly line sitting on top of the third line of the staff.

- Eighth Rest: Indicates half a beat of silence and is represented by a squiggly line attached to a stem.

- Sixteenth Rest: Indicates a quarter of a beat of silence and looks like a tiny squiggly line attached to a stem.

4. Time Signatures:

- Time signatures are written at the beginning of a piece of music and consist of two numbers stacked on top of each other.

- The top number indicates the number of beats per measure, while the bottom number indicates the type of note that receives one beat.

- Common time signatures include 4/4 (four beats per measure, quarter note receives one beat), 3/4 (three beats per measure, quarter note receives one beat), and 2/4 (two beats per measure, quarter note receives one beat).

5. Understanding Time Signatures:

- In 4/4 time, each measure contains four beats, typically divided into four quarter notes.

- In 3/4 time, each measure contains three beats, typically divided into three quarter notes.

- In 2/4 time, each measure contains two beats, typically divided into two quarter notes.

6. Counting Rhythms:

- Counting out loud or silently is essential for mastering rhythms. Use numbers to count each beat in the measure, emphasizing the first beat of each measure.

- For example, in 4/4 time, count "1, 2, 3, 4" for each measure, with each number corresponding to a quarter note beat.

By understanding rhythms and time signatures, you'll be better equipped to read and interpret written music for the cornet. Practice clapping rhythms, counting out loud, and playing along with recordings to reinforce your understanding and develop your rhythmic skills.

Reading notes on the staff is fundamental for playing music on the cornet.

1. The Staff:

- The staff consists of five horizontal lines and four spaces between the lines.

- Each line and space represents a different pitch.

2. Treble Clef:

- The treble clef is the most common clef used for cornet music.

- The treble clef symbol indicates that the second line from the bottom of the staff represents the note G above middle C.

3. Note Placement:

- Notes are placed on the lines and spaces of the staff to represent different pitches.

- The higher a note is positioned on the staff, the higher its pitch.

4. Letter Names of Notes:

- The notes on the lines of the treble clef staff, from bottom to top, are E, G, B, D, and F (remembered with the mnemonic "Every Good Boy Deserves Fudge").

  - The notes in the spaces of the treble clef staff, from bottom to top, are F, A, C, and E (remembered with the mnemonic "FACE").

5. Ledger Lines:

  - Notes that fall above or below the staff are indicated by ledger lines, which are short lines placed above or below the staff lines.

  - Ledger lines extend the staff to accommodate notes that are higher or lower than the usual range of the instrument.

6. Note Duration:

  - In addition to representing pitch, notes also indicate duration or length of time.

- Different types of notes have different durations, which are determined by their shape and associated with counts or beats.

7. Reading Notes:

- Practice identifying and naming notes on the staff using a music notation guide or flashcards.

- Start by focusing on the notes within the range of the cornet and gradually expand your knowledge to include ledger lines and higher or lower notes.

8. Repetition and Practice:

- Repetition is key to becoming fluent in reading notes on the staff.

- Practice reading simple melodies, exercises, and etudes, and gradually increase the difficulty as your skills improve.

By understanding how notes are represented on the staff and practicing regularly, you'll develop the ability to read and interpret written music for the cornet with confidence and accuracy. Start with the basics and gradually build your knowledge and proficiency over time.

Chapter 6

Beginning Repertoire

Easy Songs and Melodies to Practice

As you embark on your journey of learning the cornet, it's essential to start with simple and accessible pieces to build your skills and confidence. Here are some easy songs and melodies that are perfect for beginners to practice:

1. "Hot Cross Buns":

   - This traditional nursery rhyme is an excellent choice for beginners due to its simple melody and repetitive nature.

   - Practice playing the melody slowly and evenly, focusing on achieving a clear and consistent tone on each note.

2. "Mary Had a Little Lamb":

- Another classic nursery rhyme, "Mary Had a Little Lamb" is a great tune for beginners to practice.

   - Focus on playing the melody with smooth phrasing and correct rhythm, paying attention to dynamics and articulation.

3. "Twinkle, Twinkle, Little Star":

   - The familiar melody of "Twinkle, Twinkle, Little Star" makes it an ideal piece for beginners to learn.

   - Practice playing the melody with a gentle, singing tone, and experiment with adding dynamics and expression to enhance the musicality of the piece.

4. "Ode to Joy" (from Beethoven's Symphony No. 9):

- The iconic theme from Beethoven's Symphony No. 9, "Ode to Joy," is a timeless melody that is accessible to beginners.

- Start by learning the main melody, focusing on playing each note with clarity and precision.

5. "Aura Lee" (also known as "Love Me Tender"):

- This well-known folk melody is simple yet beautiful, making it an excellent choice for beginners to practice.

- Pay attention to the phrasing and expression of the melody, aiming to convey the gentle and heartfelt character of the piece.

6. "When the Saints Go Marching In":

- This popular traditional tune is fun and upbeat, making it a great choice for beginners to practice rhythm and articulation.

- Experiment with playing the melody in different styles, such as swing or march, to develop versatility and musical interpretation.

7. "Jingle Bells":

- "Jingle Bells" is a festive and joyous tune that is perfect for beginners to practice during the holiday season.

- Focus on playing the melody with a light and playful touch, and have fun experimenting with different tempos and dynamics.

8. "London Bridge Is Falling Down":

- This lively and energetic nursery rhyme is a great piece for beginners to practice rhythm and coordination.

- Pay attention to the steady pulse and precise articulation of the melody, and have fun with the playful character of the piece.

These easy songs and melodies provide a solid foundation for beginners to develop their skills and musicality on the cornet. Start with simple pieces like these and gradually progress to more challenging repertoire as you become more confident and proficient on the instrument. Remember to practice regularly and enjoy the process of making music!

Here are the notes for each of the mentioned easy songs and melodies:

1. "Hot Cross Buns":

   - E D C - E D C - C C C C - D D D D - E E E E - E D C

2. "Mary Had a Little Lamb":

   - E D C D E E E - D D D - E G G - E D C D E E E - E D D E D C

3. "Twinkle, Twinkle, Little Star":

- C C G G A A G - F F E E D D C - G G F F E E D - G G F F E E D - C C G G A A G - F F E E D D C

4. "Ode to Joy" (from Beethoven's Symphony No. 9):

- E E F G G F E D C C D E E D D - E F G G F E D C C D E D C

5. "Aura Lee" (also known as "Love Me Tender"):

- E E D C D E - E E D C E E - D G - E E D C D E - E E D C E D C

6. "When the Saints Go Marching In":

- E G F E D C - E G F E D E - E E F G A G - E E D C D E

7. "Jingle Bells":

- E E E - E E E - E G C D E - F F F F - F E E E - E D D E - D G G - E E E - E E E - E G C D E - F F E E - F E D C

8. "London Bridge Is Falling Down":

- G G A G F E - D D E D C B - A A G - B B A - G G F E F E D C B - G G A G F E - D D E D C B - A A G - B B A - G G F E F E D C B

Improving tone and technique on the cornet requires consistent practice and focused exercises. Here are some exercises designed to help you enhance your tone quality and technical proficiency:

1. Long Tones:

   - Play sustained notes for an extended duration, focusing on achieving a clear and resonant tone.

   - Start with comfortable pitches and gradually expand to higher and lower registers.

   - Pay attention to breath support, embouchure control, and consistent airflow throughout each note.

2. Lip Slurs:

- Practice moving between different notes in a smooth and connected manner without using the valves.

- Start with simple two-note slurs, then gradually expand to larger intervals and more complex patterns.

- Focus on maintaining a steady airflow and smooth transition between notes, using your embouchure to guide the pitch changes.

3. Articulation Exercises:

- Practice single tonguing, double tonguing, and triple tonguing exercises to improve articulation and clarity of attacks.

- Start with simple patterns and gradually increase the speed and complexity of the exercises.

- Focus on crisp and precise articulation, with each note beginning cleanly and evenly.

4. Scales and Arpeggios:

- Practice major and minor scales, as well as arpeggios, in all keys to develop finger dexterity and familiarity with different tonalities.

- Start slowly and gradually increase the speed as you become more comfortable with each scale.

- Pay attention to finger coordination, accuracy, and evenness of tone across the entire range of the instrument.

5. Interval Studies:

- Practice playing intervals (such as thirds, fourths, fifths, etc.) in various patterns and sequences.

- Focus on maintaining consistent tone and intonation while navigating different intervals and intervals.

6. Dynamic Control Exercises:

   - Practice playing exercises and melodies at different dynamic levels, ranging from pianissimo to fortissimo.

   - Experiment with crescendos, decrescendos, and sudden dynamic changes to develop control and expression in your playing.

   - Focus on maintaining a consistent tone quality and support at all dynamic levels.

7. Etudes and Studies:

   - Work on etudes and studies specifically designed to address technical challenges and musical concepts.

- Choose pieces that target areas of weakness in your playing and focus on improving specific aspects of your technique and tone production.

- Approach each etude with a clear goal in mind and practice systematically to achieve measurable progress over time.

8. Breathing Exercises:

- Practice breathing exercises to improve breath control, lung capacity, and efficiency of airflow.

- Incorporate exercises such as long, slow breaths, breath retention, and controlled exhalations to develop strength and endurance in your respiratory muscles.

Consistent and focused practice of these exercises will help you develop a strong and expressive tone, as well as enhance your technical proficiency on the cornet. Remember to practice with patience and perseverance, and don't hesitate to seek guidance from a qualified instructor for personalized feedback and instruction.

Chapter 7

Developing Skills

Intermediate Techniques for Advancing Players
For advancing players looking to elevate their cornet playing to the next level, mastering intermediate techniques is essential. Here are some key intermediate techniques to focus on:

1. Extended Range Exercises:

   - Work on expanding your range by practicing exercises that explore the upper and lower registers of the cornet.

   - Start with simple scale patterns and gradually extend into arpeggios, intervals, and melodic passages that require you to navigate through the full range of the instrument.

2. Flexibility Exercises:

- Practice flexibility exercises to improve your ability to maneuver smoothly and quickly between different notes and intervals.

- Focus on lip slurs, octave jumps, and chromatic passages that challenge your embouchure control and flexibility.

3. Multiple Tonguing Techniques:

- Expand your articulation skills by mastering multiple tonguing techniques such as double tonguing and triple tonguing.

- Practice exercises that alternate between single tonguing and multiple tonguing to improve speed, clarity, and endurance in your articulation.

4. Advanced Articulation Patterns:

- Challenge yourself with advanced articulation patterns such as staccato, legato, marcato, and accents.

- Practice these patterns in various rhythmic contexts and musical styles to develop versatility and control in your articulation.

5. Expressive Techniques:

- Explore expressive techniques such as vibrato, dynamics, phrasing, and tone color to add depth and emotion to your playing.

- Experiment with different vibrato styles, dynamic contrasts, and nuanced phrasing to enhance the musicality and expressiveness of your performances.

6. Advanced Scales and Modes:

- Dive deeper into scales and modes beyond the basic major and minor scales, including harmonic minor, melodic minor, whole-tone, and pentatonic scales.

- Practice these scales in all keys and explore their unique characteristics and applications in different musical contexts.

7. Artistic Interpretation:

  - Develop your artistic interpretation skills by studying and analyzing advanced repertoire from various musical periods and styles.

  - Explore different interpretations of the same piece, and experiment with phrasing, tempo, dynamics, and expressive nuances to develop your own artistic voice.

8. Performance Preparation:

  - Prepare for performances by practicing mock auditions, recitals, and competitions to build confidence and poise under pressure.

- Record yourself regularly to evaluate your performance objectively and identify areas for improvement.

By focusing on these intermediate techniques and practicing consistently with dedication and perseverance, you'll continue to advance and grow as a cornet player. Remember to set specific goals, seek feedback from instructors or mentors, and maintain a disciplined practice routine to maximize your progress and achieve your musical aspirations.

Practicing effectively is crucial for improving your skills on the cornet:

1. Set Clear Goals:

   - Define specific and achievable goals for each practice session. Whether it's mastering a particular technique, learning a new piece, or improving a challenging passage, having clear objectives will help keep you focused and motivated.

2. Establish a Routine:

   - Create a consistent practice routine and schedule regular practice sessions throughout the week. Aim for shorter, focused sessions rather than long, unfocused ones. Consistency is key to making steady progress over time.

3. Warm Up Properly:

   - Start each practice session with a thorough warm-up routine to prepare your body and mind for playing. Incorporate breathing exercises, lip slurs, and scales to warm up your muscles, improve flexibility, and establish good habits from the outset.

4. Focus on Technique:

- Dedicate time to practicing fundamental techniques such as tone production, articulation, finger dexterity, and breath control. Break down challenging passages into smaller components and work on them gradually to build proficiency and accuracy.

5. Use a Metronome:

   - Practice with a metronome to develop a strong sense of rhythm, timing, and pulse. Start at a comfortable tempo and gradually increase the speed as you become more comfortable with the passage. Playing with a metronome will also help improve your overall sense of timing and coordination.

6. Practice Mindfully:

   - Practice with full concentration and mindfulness, focusing on the quality of your sound, technique, and musical expression. Avoid mindless repetition and strive for deliberate, purposeful practice with attention to detail.

7. Record Yourself:

  - Record yourself regularly during practice sessions to assess your progress objectively. Listen back to your recordings and identify areas for improvement, such as intonation, articulation, dynamics, and phrasing. Recording yourself provides valuable feedback and helps track your development over time.

8. Take Breaks:

  - Take regular breaks during practice sessions to rest your muscles and prevent fatigue. Short breaks every 20-30 minutes can help maintain focus and prevent burnout. Use break time to stretch, hydrate, and relax before returning to your practice session refreshed.

9. Stay Positive and Patient:

- Stay positive and patient with yourself throughout the learning process. Recognize that progress takes time and effort, and celebrate small victories along the way. Embrace mistakes as opportunities for growth and learning, and maintain a positive attitude even during challenging practice sessions.

10. Seek Feedback:

  - Seek feedback from teachers, mentors, or fellow musicians to gain valuable insights and guidance. Take advantage of opportunities for private lessons, masterclasses, and group rehearsals to receive constructive criticism and learn from others' experiences.

By incorporating these tips into your practice routine, you'll be able to practice more effectively and efficiently, leading to steady improvement and growth as a cornet player. Remember to stay patient, persistent, and proactive in your approach to practice, and enjoy the journey of learning and mastering the instrument.

Introducing more complex musical pieces into your repertoire can be both exciting and challenging. Here's a guide to help you navigate and approach these pieces effectively:

1. Selecting Pieces:

   - Choose pieces that are slightly above your current skill level to challenge yourself and facilitate growth.

   - Consider factors such as technical demands, range, rhythm complexity, and musical expression when selecting pieces.

2. Score Study:

   - Begin by studying the score of the piece thoroughly, paying attention to key signatures, time signatures, tempo markings, dynamics, articulations, and any other markings that provide insight into the composer's intentions.

- Analyze the overall structure of the piece, identifying sections, phrases, and thematic material.

3. Practice Strategies:

- Break down the piece into manageable sections and prioritize areas that require the most work.

- Practice each section slowly and systematically, focusing on accuracy, clarity, and musicality.

- Use practice techniques such as rhythmic subdivision, slow practice, and incremental tempo increases to master difficult passages.

4. Technical Challenges:

- Identify technical challenges within the piece, such as fast passages, intricate rhythms, and complex articulations.

- Practice technical exercises and drills targeted at specific challenges to improve your proficiency and confidence in executing these passages.

5. Musical Expression:

- Explore the musicality of the piece by experimenting with different interpretations, phrasing options, and expressive nuances.

- Consider the character, mood, and emotion conveyed by the music, and strive to bring these elements to life in your performance.

6. Listening and Analysis:

- Listen to recordings of professional performances of the piece to gain insight into interpretive choices and stylistic conventions.

- Analyze multiple interpretations of the same piece to broaden your understanding of its musical possibilities and develop your own artistic voice.

7. Practice Efficiency:

- Practice efficiently by focusing on areas of weakness and prioritizing your time and energy on tasks that will yield the most improvement.

- Set specific practice goals for each session and track your progress to ensure consistent growth and development.

8. Performance Preparation:

- Prepare for performances by rehearsing with accompaniment, practicing in performance conditions, and simulating the experience of playing for an audience.

- Work on memorization, stage presence, and mental preparation to build confidence and poise for public performances.

By approaching more complex musical pieces with careful preparation, focused practice, and a commitment to musical expression, you'll be able to tackle challenging repertoire with confidence and proficiency. Remember to be patient and persistent in your practice, and enjoy the process of learning and mastering these exciting musical works.

Chapter 8

Cornet Maintenance
Cleaning and Caring for Your Instrument

Proper maintenance is essential for keeping your cornet in optimal condition and ensuring its longevity. Here's a comprehensive guide to cleaning and caring for your instrument:

1. Daily Maintenance Routine:

   - After each practice session or performance, wipe down the exterior of your cornet with a clean, dry cloth to remove any moisture, fingerprints, or oils that may have accumulated.

   - Pay special attention to the areas where your hands come into contact with the instrument, such as the valves, valve casings, and slides.

2. Valve Maintenance:

- Regularly oil the valves using valve oil recommended by your instrument manufacturer. Apply a few drops of oil to each valve and work the valve up and down to distribute the oil evenly.

- Avoid over-oiling the valves, as excessive oil can lead to sluggish valve action and buildup of residue.

3. Slide Maintenance:

- Check the slides of your cornet regularly to ensure they move freely and smoothly. If a slide becomes stuck or difficult to move, apply a small amount of slide grease to lubricate it.

- Clean the slides periodically by removing them from the instrument and wiping them down with a clean cloth. Avoid using excessive force when removing or reinserting slides to prevent damage to the instrument.

4. Cleaning the Interior:

   - Periodically clean the interior of your cornet to remove any dirt, debris, or residue that may have accumulated.

   - Use a cleaning snake or flexible brush designed for brass instruments to clean out the tubing and remove any obstructions.

   - Rinse the interior of the instrument with lukewarm water to flush out any remaining debris, then dry thoroughly with a clean, lint-free cloth.

5. Polishing:

   - Polish the exterior of your cornet periodically to remove tarnish and restore its luster. Use a polishing cloth or brass polish recommended for use on musical instruments.

   - Avoid abrasive polishes or cleaning agents that may damage the finish of the instrument, and always follow the manufacturer's instructions for proper use.

6. Storage:

 - Store your cornet in a protective case when not in use to shield it from dust, moisture, and potential damage.

 - Avoid exposing your instrument to extreme temperatures or humidity, as this can cause damage to the finish, valves, and other components.

 - Store your cornet in an upright position to prevent stress on the valves and slides.

7. Professional Maintenance:

 - Schedule regular maintenance check-ups with a qualified instrument technician to ensure that your cornet is in good working condition.

- A professional technician can perform thorough cleaning, lubrication, adjustment, and repairs as needed to keep your instrument performing at its best.

By following these guidelines for cleaning and caring for your cornet, you'll prolong its lifespan, maintain its playability, and preserve its appearance for years to come. Regular maintenance is key to keeping your instrument in top condition and ensuring that you can continue to enjoy playing it for many years.

Troubleshooting common issues with your cornet can help you address problems quickly and prevent further damage.

1. Stuck Valves:

  - If your valves become stuck or sluggish, first check if they are properly lubricated. Apply valve oil to each valve and work them up and down to distribute the oil evenly.

   - If the valves remain stuck, avoid forcing them. Instead, gently tap the valve caps with the palm of your hand or use a rubber mallet to loosen them.

   - If the problem persists, seek assistance from a qualified instrument technician to diagnose and resolve the issue.

2. Air Leaks:

   - Air leaks can occur at various points in the instrument, including the valve casings, slides, and solder joints.

   - Check for visible signs of damage or misalignment, such as gaps or cracks in the tubing, and address them promptly.

- Apply slide grease to slides that do not seal properly and ensure that all valves and slides are properly seated and aligned.

3. Intonation Issues:

   - If you experience intonation problems, such as notes that are consistently sharp or flat, check your embouchure and air support first.

   - Experiment with adjusting your embouchure, breath support, and mouthpiece placement to correct intonation issues.

   - If intonation problems persist, consult a teacher or experienced player for guidance on proper technique and adjustment.

4. Sticky Slides:

   - Sticky slides can be caused by a buildup of dirt, debris, or residue inside the tubing.

- Clean the slides thoroughly using a cleaning snake or flexible brush designed for brass instruments, and rinse with lukewarm water to remove any remaining debris.

- Apply slide grease to the cleaned slides to lubricate them and ensure smooth movement.

5. Dented or Damaged Parts:

- If you notice dents, dings, or other damage to your cornet, handle the instrument with care to prevent further damage.

- Consult a qualified instrument technician for repair or replacement of damaged parts, such as bent slides, dented tubing, or loose solder joints.

- Avoid attempting repairs yourself, as improper handling can cause additional damage to the instrument.

6. Loss of Compression:

- Loss of compression can result from worn valve felts, worn valve guides, or damaged valve springs.

- Check the condition of the valve felts, guides, and springs, and replace any worn or damaged components as needed.

- Ensure that valves are properly lubricated and seated to maintain a tight seal and prevent air leakage.

7. Mouthpiece Fit:

- If you experience difficulty inserting or removing the mouthpiece, check for dirt, debris, or corrosion inside the receiver.

- Clean the mouthpiece receiver with a soft cloth or brush, and apply a small amount of valve oil or grease to lubricate it if necessary.

- Avoid using excessive force when inserting or removing the mouthpiece to prevent damage to the instrument.

By addressing common issues promptly and effectively, you can keep your cornet in good working condition and ensure that it performs at its best. If you encounter persistent problems or are unsure how to resolve an issue, don't hesitate to seek assistance from a qualified instrument technician.

Knowing when to seek professional maintenance for your cornet is essential for keeping it in optimal playing condition.

1. Valve Issues:

   - If your valves are consistently sticky, sluggish, or difficult to move despite proper lubrication, it may indicate a more serious problem with the valve mechanism.

- Seek professional maintenance if your valves become stuck or if you notice excessive wear on the valve pistons or casing.

2. Air Leaks:

  - If you experience air leaks in the instrument, such as a noticeable loss of compression or a hissing sound when playing, it may indicate leaks in the valve casings, slides, or solder joints.

  - Seek professional maintenance to identify and repair any leaks, as they can affect the instrument's playability and sound quality.

3. Intonation Issues:

  - If you encounter persistent intonation problems, such as notes that are consistently sharp or flat across the instrument's range, it may indicate issues with the alignment or condition of the tubing.

- Seek professional maintenance to address intonation issues and ensure that the instrument is properly adjusted and regulated.

4. Physical Damage:

  - If your cornet sustains physical damage, such as dents, dings, or bent slides, it's important to have it inspected by a qualified technician.

  - Even minor damage can affect the instrument's playability and sound quality, so it's best to address any issues promptly to prevent further damage.

5. Routine Maintenance:

  - Regular maintenance is essential for keeping your cornet in good working condition. If it's been more than a year since your last maintenance check-up, or if you notice any signs of wear or deterioration, it's a good idea to schedule a professional inspection and cleaning.

- A qualified technician can perform thorough maintenance, including cleaning, lubrication, adjustment, and repair as needed, to ensure that your cornet performs at its best.

6. Unusual Noises or Vibrations:

- If you notice any unusual noises, vibrations, or rattling sounds when playing your cornet, it may indicate loose parts, worn components, or other mechanical issues.

- Seek professional maintenance to diagnose and address any mechanical problems to prevent further damage to the instrument.

7. Difficulty Playing:

- If you experience difficulty playing the instrument, such as uneven response, poor tone quality, or limited range, it may indicate underlying mechanical issues that require professional attention.

- Seek assistance from a qualified technician to diagnose and resolve any playing problems and ensure that your cornet is functioning properly.

By being proactive and attentive to the condition of your cornet, you can ensure that it remains in optimal playing condition and continues to bring you joy for years to come. Regular maintenance and timely repairs are essential for preserving the integrity and performance of your instrument, so don't hesitate to seek professional assistance when needed.

Chapter 9

Playing with Others
Joining a Brass Ensemble or Band

Joining a brass ensemble or band can be an enriching and rewarding experience for cornet players. Here's a guide to help you navigate this exciting opportunity:

1. Finding a Brass Ensemble or Band:

   - Research local brass ensembles, concert bands, wind ensembles, or community bands in your area.

   - Check local music schools, community centers, or online directories for information on auditions, rehearsals, and performance opportunities.

2. Preparing for Auditions:

- If auditions are required, prepare by practicing scales, sight-reading, and prepared excerpts as specified by the ensemble.

- Familiarize yourself with the ensemble's repertoire and style to align your playing with their musical goals and expectations.

3. Attending Rehearsals:

- Once accepted into a brass ensemble or band, attend rehearsals regularly and punctually.

- Be attentive and respectful during rehearsals, and follow the conductor's instructions and musical interpretations.

4. Collaborating with Other Musicians:

- Embrace the collaborative nature of ensemble playing by listening actively to other musicians and adjusting your playing to blend and balance with the group.

- Practice ensemble skills such as intonation, balance, dynamics, and rhythmic precision to enhance the overall sound of the ensemble.

5. Learning New Repertoire:

- Embrace the opportunity to learn new repertoire and musical styles by actively engaging with the ensemble's music selection.

- Practice your parts independently to ensure preparedness for rehearsals and performances.

6. Developing Musical Skills:

- Playing in a brass ensemble or band provides valuable experience in ensemble skills, musical interpretation, and performance etiquette.

- Take advantage of the opportunity to develop your musical skills, including sight-reading, listening, and responding to musical cues from fellow musicians.

7. Building Camaraderie and Teamwork:

   - Foster a sense of camaraderie and teamwork within the ensemble by building positive relationships with fellow musicians.

   - Support and encourage each other during rehearsals and performances, and celebrate collective achievements as a group.

8. Preparing for Performances:

   - Prepare diligently for ensemble performances by practicing individually and attending all scheduled rehearsals.

   - Focus on musical expression, precision, and unity with the ensemble to deliver polished and engaging performances.

9. Enjoying the Experience:

- Above all, enjoy the experience of playing music with others and sharing your passion for the cornet.

- Embrace the challenges and rewards of ensemble playing, and cherish the opportunity to contribute to the musical community through collaborative performances.

Joining a brass ensemble or band is a wonderful way to enhance your musical skills, expand your repertoire, and connect with fellow musicians. Embrace the experience with enthusiasm and dedication, and savor the joy of making music together as part of a cohesive ensemble.

Observing proper etiquette during group rehearsals and performances is essential for maintaining a positive and productive musical environment.

1. Arrive on Time:

- Arrive punctually for rehearsals and performances to allow ample time for setup, tuning, and preparation.

- Prompt arrival demonstrates respect for your fellow musicians and ensures that rehearsals start promptly and run smoothly.

2. Come Prepared:

- Come to rehearsals and performances prepared with all necessary materials, including sheet music, a pencil for marking parts, and any required accessories or equipment.

- Practice your parts independently beforehand to minimize disruptions and maximize rehearsal efficiency.

3. Respect the Conductor:

- Respect the authority of the conductor and follow their instructions and musical interpretations.

- Pay attention to verbal cues, gestures, and visual cues from the conductor, and respond promptly and attentively to their direction.

4. Listen Actively:

- Listen attentively to other musicians during rehearsals and performances, and adjust your playing to blend and balance with the ensemble.

- Be receptive to feedback from the conductor and fellow musicians, and strive to implement constructive criticism to improve your performance.

5. Maintain Focus:

- Maintain focus and concentration during rehearsals and performances, avoiding distractions such as talking, texting, or browsing on electronic devices.

- Stay engaged in the music-making process and avoid disruptive behavior that detracts from the rehearsal or performance experience.

6. Be Supportive:

- Foster a supportive and collaborative atmosphere within the ensemble by encouraging and acknowledging the contributions of fellow musicians.

- Offer assistance or guidance to less experienced musicians when appropriate, and celebrate collective achievements as a group.

7. Respect Instruments and Equipment:

- Handle instruments and equipment with care to prevent damage or injury.

- Avoid placing instruments or equipment in precarious positions or leaving them unattended where they may be at risk of damage.

8. Communicate Effectively:

- Communicate respectfully and professionally with fellow musicians, the conductor, and any other personnel involved in rehearsals and performances.

- Address concerns or conflicts directly and diplomatically, and work together to find mutually acceptable solutions.

9. Show Appreciation:

- Show appreciation and gratitude to the conductor, fellow musicians, and any support staff or volunteers involved in rehearsals and performances.

- Express thanks for their contributions and efforts, both individually and collectively, to foster a positive and inclusive musical community.

By observing proper etiquette during group rehearsals and performances, you contribute to a harmonious and productive musical environment that enhances the rehearsal and performance experience for everyone involved.

Playing in tune with others is essential for creating a cohesive and harmonious ensemble sound. Here are some tips to help you play in tune with your fellow musicians:

1. Listen and Adjust:

   - Listen attentively to the sound of the ensemble and adjust your pitch to blend and match with the group.

   - Develop your ear-training skills by practicing listening to and imitating pitch accurately.

2. Tune Before Rehearsals:

   - Tune your instrument before rehearsals and performances to ensure that you start from a consistent pitch reference.

   - Use a tuner or tuning app to ensure accuracy, and check your tuning periodically throughout rehearsals as the temperature and humidity may affect pitch.

3. Be Aware of Intonation Challenges:

   - Be mindful of common intonation challenges in brass instruments, such as wide intervals, harmonic series tendencies, and register transitions.

   - Practice passages with challenging intervals or harmonic relationships to develop muscle memory and intonation awareness.

4. Adjust Embouchure and Air Support:

- Experiment with your embouchure and air support to find the optimal position and pressure for producing in-tune notes.

- Focus on supporting the pitch with steady airflow and a firm, yet flexible embouchure, especially in the upper register.

5. Use Harmonic Series Fingerings:

- Use alternate fingerings or slide positions based on the harmonic series to adjust pitch and improve intonation, particularly in the lower register.

- Practice scales and exercises using different fingerings to develop fluency and flexibility in adjusting pitch as needed.

6. Match Articulation and Attack:

- Match your articulation and attack with that of the ensemble to ensure uniformity and clarity of sound.

- Pay attention to the conductor's cues and follow their direction regarding articulation, dynamics, and phrasing.

7. Listen to Section Leaders:

- Listen to section leaders or principal players for guidance on pitch, intonation, and musical interpretation.

- Follow their lead and adjust your playing to align with the section's sound and blend seamlessly with the ensemble.

8. Practice Tuning Drills:

- Practice tuning drills and exercises with the ensemble to develop a shared sense of pitch and intonation.

- Experiment with tuning drones or sustained tones to establish a reference pitch and practice adjusting your pitch to match.

9. Record and Listen Back:

  - Record ensemble rehearsals and performances to assess intonation and identify areas for improvement.

  - Listen back to recordings critically and analyze intonation discrepancies, then work on addressing these issues in subsequent rehearsals.

10. Seek Feedback:

  - Seek feedback from fellow musicians, section leaders, and the conductor on intonation and pitch.

  - Be open to constructive criticism and use feedback to refine your intonation skills and contribute positively to the ensemble sound.

By implementing these tips and practicing consistently with a focus on intonation, you'll develop the skills and sensitivity needed to play in tune with others effectively. Remember that playing in tune is a collaborative effort that requires active listening, adjustment, and communication within the ensemble.

Chapter 10

Cornet in Different Musical Genres
Exploring the Versatility of the Cornet

The cornet is a versatile instrument capable of lending its distinctive sound to a wide range of musical genres. Here's a look at how the cornet can be utilized in various musical styles:

1. Classical Music:

   - In classical music, the cornet is often featured in orchestral, chamber, and solo repertoire.

   - It has a rich tradition in brass band music, where it is used as both a solo and ensemble instrument, particularly in British brass band repertoire.

   - In orchestral settings, the cornet is occasionally called upon to play solo passages or add color and texture to brass sections.

2. Jazz:

   - The cornet has a prominent role in traditional jazz and Dixieland music, where it is often used as a lead instrument in front-line ensembles.

   - Jazz cornetists, such as Louis Armstrong and Bix Beiderbecke, helped popularize the instrument in the early 20th century with their virtuosic improvisations and expressive playing styles.

   - The cornet's warm, mellow tone and agility make it well-suited for melodic improvisation and ensemble playing in jazz settings.

3. Blues:

   - In blues music, the cornet can add a soulful and emotive quality to performances.

   - Cornetists in blues bands may play melodic lines, fills, or solos, contributing to the overall sound and feel of the music.

- The cornet's ability to bend notes and add expressive nuances makes it an effective instrument for conveying the raw emotion and intensity of the blues.

4. Marching Bands:

   - The cornet is a staple instrument in marching bands, where it is used to provide melodic and harmonic support in outdoor performances.

   - In marching band arrangements, cornets often play a mix of traditional marches, popular tunes, and original compositions tailored for the ensemble's instrumentation and style.

5. Brass Ensembles:

   - In brass ensembles, the cornet serves as a versatile voice, capable of blending with other brass instruments or standing out as a soloist.

- Brass ensembles may perform a diverse repertoire spanning classical, jazz, pop, and contemporary music, showcasing the cornet's adaptability across different genres.

6. Pop and Rock Music:

   - While less common than in other genres, the cornet can be found in pop and rock music settings, adding a unique color and texture to arrangements.

   - In pop and rock bands, the cornet may be used for melodic hooks, solos, or background embellishments, contributing to the overall sonic palette of the ensemble.

7. World Music:

   - In various world music traditions, the cornet may be adapted or incorporated into indigenous musical styles, lending a Western brass flavor to traditional sounds.

- Cornetists may explore fusion projects or collaborations with musicians from different cultural backgrounds, blending the instrument's versatility with diverse musical influences.

The cornet's versatility allows it to thrive in a wide array of musical genres, from classical and jazz to blues, marching bands, pop, rock, and beyond. Whether performing as a soloist, ensemble member, or session musician, the cornet adds a distinctive and expressive voice to any musical setting, enriching the listening experience for audiences worldwide.

The cornet plays a diverse role across different musical genres, showcasing its versatility and adaptability to various styles of music:

1. Jazz:

   - In jazz, the cornet holds a prominent position, particularly in traditional jazz and Dixieland bands.

- Cornetists in jazz ensembles often serve as lead instrumentalists, delivering melodic lines, improvisations, and solos with flair and expressiveness.

- The cornet's warm, mellow tone and agility make it well-suited for navigating the complex harmonies and syncopated rhythms of jazz music.

- Jazz cornetists, such as Louis Armstrong, Bix Beiderbecke, and King Oliver, have left an indelible mark on the genre with their innovative playing styles and virtuosic improvisations.

2. Classical:

- In classical music, the cornet has a diverse role, appearing in orchestral, chamber, and solo repertoire.

- While less common than the trumpet, the cornet occasionally features as a solo instrument in orchestral works, adding color and texture to brass sections.

- In brass band music, particularly in British brass bands, the cornet holds a central role, serving as both a soloist and ensemble player. Its agile and lyrical qualities are showcased in a wide range of traditional and contemporary brass band compositions.

3. Marching Bands:

- The cornet is a staple instrument in marching bands, where it contributes to the melodic and harmonic fabric of outdoor performances.

- In marching band arrangements, cornets play a variety of roles, from carrying the melody to providing harmonic support and adding embellishments and flourishes.

- Cornet sections in marching bands often feature prominently in parade marches, halftime shows, and other public performances, projecting a powerful and dynamic sound that captivates audiences.

4. Brass Ensembles:

   - In brass ensembles, the cornet serves as a versatile voice, capable of blending with other brass instruments or standing out as a soloist.

   - Brass ensembles may feature cornets in a variety of configurations, from small chamber groups to large orchestral-style ensembles, showcasing the instrument's adaptability across different musical styles and genres.

5. Pop and Rock Music:

   - While less common than in jazz or classical music, the cornet can be found in pop and rock bands, adding a unique brass flavor to arrangements.

- In pop and rock music settings, cornets may contribute melodic hooks, solos, or background embellishments, enriching the sonic palette of the ensemble and adding depth and color to the overall sound.

6. Other Genres:

  - The cornet's versatility extends to other musical genres, including blues, world music, and contemporary styles.

  - In blues bands, the cornet can add a soulful and expressive quality to performances, delivering emotive solos and melodic fills.

  - In world music traditions, the cornet may be adapted or incorporated into indigenous musical styles, blending Western brass sounds with diverse cultural influences.

In summary, the cornet's role in jazz, classical, and other genres is multifaceted, reflecting its versatility and ability to adapt to a wide range of musical contexts. Whether performing as a lead instrumentalist, ensemble player, or session musician, the cornet adds a distinctive and expressive voice to any musical setting, enriching the listening experience for audiences worldwide.

Several famous cornet players have made significant contributions to the instrument's legacy and to the genres in which it is prominently featured. Here are a few notable cornetists and their contributions:

1. Louis Armstrong (1901-1971):

   - Known as one of the most influential figures in jazz history, Louis Armstrong revolutionized jazz trumpet and cornet playing.

   - Armstrong's innovative improvisations, distinctive gravelly voice, and charismatic stage presence helped popularize jazz and elevate the role of the cornet in early jazz ensembles.

  - His recordings with the Hot Five and Hot Seven bands in the 1920s, such as "West End Blues" and "Potato Head Blues," remain seminal works in jazz history and showcase his virtuosic cornet playing.

2. Bix Beiderbecke (1903-1931):

  - Bix Beiderbecke was a pioneering jazz cornetist and composer known for his lyrical playing style and innovative approach to improvisation.

  - Beiderbecke's recordings with the Wolverines, Jean Goldkette Orchestra, and Paul Whiteman Orchestra in the 1920s helped define the jazz age and inspire generations of musicians.

  - His compositions, including "In a Mist" and "Davenport Blues," demonstrate his unique harmonic language and melodic sensibility, influencing subsequent generations of jazz musicians.

3. King Oliver (1885-1938):

   - Joe "King" Oliver was a seminal figure in early jazz and one of the first great jazz cornetists.

   - Oliver's Creole Jazz Band, featuring Louis Armstrong on second cornet, was one of the most popular and influential jazz ensembles of the 1920s.

   - His recordings, such as "Dipper Mouth Blues" and "Canal Street Blues," showcase his powerful tone, virtuosic technique, and innovative use of muted trumpet and cornet effects.

4. Wynton Marsalis (b. 1961):

   - Wynton Marsalis is a contemporary jazz trumpeter and cornetist known for his virtuosic playing, compositional prowess, and advocacy for jazz education and preservation.

- Marsalis has won numerous Grammy Awards for his recordings and compositions, which span a wide range of jazz styles from traditional to avant-garde.

- As the artistic director of Jazz at Lincoln Center, Marsalis has worked to promote jazz appreciation and education through performances, educational programs, and outreach initiatives.

5. Herbert L. Clarke (1867-1945):

- Herbert L. Clarke was a renowned cornet soloist, composer, and educator who made significant contributions to the development of brass technique and repertoire.

- Clarke's virtuosic cornet solos, such as "The Debutante" and "Bride of the Waves," are still widely performed by brass players today and are considered standard repertoire for the instrument.

- As a teacher and author, Clarke wrote several instructional books and method books that remain influential in brass pedagogy, including "Technical Studies for the Cornet" and "Character Studies for the Cornet."

These are just a few examples of famous cornet players who have left a lasting impact on the instrument and the genres in which it is featured. Their contributions to jazz, classical, and other musical styles continue to inspire musicians and audiences around the world.

Chapter 11

Performance Tips
Overcoming Stage Fright

Stage fright, also known as performance anxiety, is a common experience for many musicians, but with the right strategies, it can be managed effectively. Here are some tips to help you overcome stage fright and perform with confidence:

1. Prepare Thoroughly:

   - The more prepared you are, the more confident you'll feel on stage. Practice your repertoire diligently, focusing on technical accuracy, musical interpretation, and memorization if applicable.

   - Rehearse in performance-like conditions, such as in front of a mirror, with a recording device, or in front of friends and family, to simulate the pressure of a live performance.

2. Visualize Success:

 - Visualize yourself performing confidently and successfully on stage. Imagine the audience responding positively to your performance and envision yourself enjoying the experience.

 - Positive visualization can help alleviate anxiety and build self-assurance leading up to the performance.

3. Controlled Breathing and Relaxation Techniques:

 - Practice deep breathing and relaxation techniques to calm your nerves and reduce physical tension before going on stage.

 - Incorporate techniques such as diaphragmatic breathing, progressive muscle relaxation, and visualization exercises to promote relaxation and focus.

4. Focus on the Music:

   - Shift your focus away from yourself and onto the music you're performing. Concentrate on expressing the emotions and intentions of the music rather than worrying about your own performance.

   - Stay present in the moment and engage fully with the music, allowing it to guide your performance and transcend any self-doubt or anxiety.

5. Develop a Pre-Performance Routine:

   - Establish a pre-performance routine that helps you feel centered, focused, and prepared before taking the stage.

- Your routine might include physical warm-ups, mental visualization exercises, positive affirmations, and calming rituals to help you feel grounded and ready to perform.

6. Reframe Negative Thoughts:

  - Challenge and reframe negative thoughts and self-talk that contribute to performance anxiety. Replace self-doubt with positive affirmations and realistic, empowering beliefs about your abilities as a musician.

  - Recognize that making mistakes is a natural part of performing and an opportunity for growth rather than a reflection of your worth as a musician.

7. Embrace the Nervous Energy:

  - Acknowledge and embrace the adrenaline and nervous energy that comes with performing. Channel that energy into your performance, allowing it to fuel your passion, intensity, and focus on stage.

- Reframe nervousness as excitement and anticipation rather than fear, recognizing that it can enhance your performance and contribute to a dynamic and engaging stage presence.

8. Focus on the Audience Connection:

- Shift your focus from your internal experience to connecting with the audience. Remember that they are there to support and appreciate your performance, and their energy can be a source of encouragement and inspiration.

- Engage with the audience through eye contact, body language, and genuine expression, creating a sense of connection and rapport that enhances your performance experience.

9. Seek Professional Help if Needed:

- If stage fright significantly interferes with your ability to perform or causes excessive distress, consider seeking support from a mental health professional, performance coach, or counselor who specializes in performance anxiety.

- Professional guidance can provide personalized strategies and techniques to help you manage and overcome stage fright effectively.

By incorporating these tips into your performance preparation and mindset, you can overcome stage fright and perform with confidence, poise, and authenticity on stage. Remember that stage fright is a common experience shared by many performers, and with practice and perseverance, you can learn to manage it and thrive as a musician.

Preparing for auditions and competitions requires careful planning, focused practice, and mental preparation. Here are some tips to help you effectively prepare for auditions and competitions:

1. Know the Requirements:

   - Familiarize yourself with the audition or competition requirements, including repertoire, audition procedures, time limits, and any specific guidelines or criteria provided by the organizers.

   - Ensure that you understand the expectations for each round of the audition or competition, including repertoire selections, technical requirements, and any additional components such as sight-reading or improvisation.

2. Choose Your Repertoire Wisely:

   - Select repertoire that showcases your strengths as a musician and aligns with the requirements and expectations of the audition or competition.

- Choose pieces that demonstrate a range of technical skills, musical expression, and stylistic versatility, while also considering your own interests and artistic preferences.

3. Practice Strategically:

- Develop a structured practice plan tailored to your audition or competition goals and timeline.

- Prioritize your repertoire selections and allocate practice time effectively to ensure thorough coverage of all required material, focusing on technical challenges, musical interpretation, and performance readiness.

- Break down complex passages into smaller sections and practice them systematically, using techniques such as slow practice, repetition, and deliberate practice to build fluency and accuracy.

4. Record Yourself:

- Record yourself practicing and performing your audition or competition repertoire to assess your progress and identify areas for improvement.

- Listen critically to your recordings, paying attention to intonation, tone quality, articulation, dynamics, and overall musicality, and make adjustments accordingly.

5. Seek Feedback:

- Solicit feedback from teachers, mentors, peers, or trusted colleagues to gain valuable insights and perspectives on your preparation and performance.

- Participate in mock auditions or competitions, either informally with friends and classmates or through organized events or workshops, to simulate the audition experience and receive constructive feedback.

6. Mental Preparation:

- Develop mental strategies to manage performance anxiety and maintain focus and confidence during auditions or competitions.

- Practice relaxation techniques such as deep breathing, visualization, and positive self-talk to calm nerves and promote a positive mindset leading up to and during the audition or competition.

7. Mock Auditions:

- Simulate audition conditions as closely as possible by organizing mock auditions with friends, teachers, or colleagues.

- Practice performing your audition repertoire in front of a small audience, mimicking the pressure and scrutiny of a real audition, and use the experience to build confidence and resilience.

8. Physical Preparation:

- Take care of your physical health and well-being leading up to the audition or competition by getting adequate rest, staying hydrated, and maintaining a balanced diet.

- Engage in regular physical exercise, such as stretching, yoga, or light cardio, to reduce tension and promote relaxation and focus.

9. Plan Your Logistics:

- Plan and organize logistical details such as transportation, lodging, and scheduling well in advance of the audition or competition date.

- Arrive early on the day of the audition or competition to allow ample time for warm-up, acclimation to the venue, and mental preparation.

10. Stay Flexible and Adapt:

- Be flexible and adaptable in your preparation and performance, remaining open to adjustments and changes as needed.

- Trust in your preparation and focus on delivering your best performance in the moment, regardless of external factors or unexpected challenges.

By following these tips and strategies, you can effectively prepare for auditions and competitions, maximize your performance potential, and present yourself with confidence and poise on stage. Remember to approach the process with dedication, focus, and a positive attitude, and trust in your abilities as a musician.

Delivering a polished performance requires meticulous preparation, confident execution, and thoughtful communication with your audience.

Here are some pieces of advice to help you deliver a polished and memorable performance:

1. Thorough Preparation:

   - Prepare your repertoire thoroughly, ensuring that you have mastered the technical demands, musical nuances, and expressive elements of each piece.

   - Practice consistently and strategically, focusing on areas of weakness and refining your interpretation to achieve a polished and confident performance.

2. Attention to Detail:

   - Pay close attention to detail in every aspect of your performance, including intonation, articulation, dynamics, phrasing, and musical expression.

- Aim for precision and clarity in your execution, striving for a flawless and polished presentation that captivates your audience.

3. Expressive Interpretation:

  - Infuse your performance with emotion, passion, and authenticity, connecting deeply with the music and conveying its expressive content to your audience.

  - Explore the subtleties of interpretation, using dynamics, articulation, and tone color to convey the nuances of the music and engage your listeners on a profound emotional level.

4. Confident Stage Presence:

  - Project confidence and poise on stage, embodying a strong and assured stage presence that commands attention and respect from your audience.

- Maintain good posture, eye contact, and body language, conveying professionalism and confidence throughout your performance.

5. Engage with Your Audience:

 - Establish a rapport with your audience through genuine and meaningful communication, connecting with them on a personal level and inviting them into your musical world.

 - Share insights into the repertoire, composers, and historical context of the music, creating a deeper appreciation and understanding of the music you're performing.

6. Adaptability and Resilience:

 - Stay adaptable and resilient in the face of unexpected challenges or distractions that may arise during your performance.

- Maintain focus and composure, responding calmly and confidently to any unforeseen circumstances while remaining committed to delivering a polished and memorable performance.

7. Embrace the Moment:

  - Embrace the opportunity to share your passion and talent with your audience, savoring the experience of performing live and celebrating the joy of making music.

  - Stay present in the moment, fully immersing yourself in the music and the connection you share with your audience, and allowing yourself to express your true artistic voice.

8. Reflect and Learn:

  - After your performance, take time to reflect on your experience and evaluate your strengths and areas for improvement.

- Seek feedback from trusted mentors, colleagues, or audience members to gain valuable insights and perspectives that can inform your growth as a performer.

By following these pieces of advice and approaching your performance with dedication, focus, and passion, you can deliver a polished and memorable performance that resonates with your audience and leaves a lasting impression. Remember to embrace the opportunity to share your music with others and to always strive for excellence in your artistic endeavors.

Chapter 12

Conclusion

Recap of Key Points

Throughout this book, we've explored the fundamentals of playing the cornet and the essential skills needed to become a proficient musician. Here's a recap of the key points covered:

1. Introduction to the Cornet:

   - We delved into the history and significance of the cornet, tracing its evolution and contributions to various musical genres.

2. Getting Started:

   - We covered the basics of the cornet, including its parts, assembly, and care, to ensure that you start your musical journey on the right note.

3. Posture and Breathing:

- We discussed the importance of proper posture and breathing techniques for optimal playing and explored exercises to improve breath control.

4. Embouchure and Mouthpiece:

- We examined the concept of embouchure and provided guidance on forming a correct embouchure and selecting the right mouthpiece for your needs.

5. Basic Techniques:

- We covered essential techniques such as holding the cornet correctly, producing your first sound, and learning simple notes and scales to build a solid foundation.

6. Music Theory Basics:

- We introduced music notation, rhythms, time signatures, and reading notes on the staff to help you understand the language of music.

7. Beginning Repertoire:

- We provided a selection of easy songs and melodies to practice, allowing you to apply your newfound skills in a musical context.

8. Developing Skills:

- We explored intermediate techniques for advancing players, offered tips for effective practice, and introduced more complex musical pieces to challenge your abilities.

9. Cornet Maintenance:

- We discussed the importance of cleaning and caring for your instrument, troubleshooting common issues, and knowing when to seek professional maintenance.

10. Playing with Others:

   - We highlighted the benefits of joining a brass ensemble or band and provided guidance on etiquette, collaboration, and performance etiquette.

11. Cornet in Different Musical Genres:

   - We explored the versatility of the cornet across various musical genres, from jazz and classical to pop, rock, and beyond, celebrating its adaptability and expressive potential.

12. Performance Tips:

   - We offered advice for overcoming stage fright, preparing for auditions and competitions, and delivering polished performances that captivate and inspire your audience.

As you continue your journey with the cornet, remember to practice regularly, stay open to learning and growth, and most importantly, enjoy the process of making music. With dedication, passion, and perseverance, you'll continue to develop your skills and share your musical talents with the world.

As you conclude this journey with the cornet, I want to offer you words of encouragement to continue learning and exploring music. Learning an instrument is a lifelong journey filled with discovery, growth, and joy. Here are some reasons to keep pursuing your musical passion:

1. Personal Growth: Learning music challenges your mind, sharpens your focus, and enhances your cognitive abilities. It fosters discipline, perseverance, and problem-solving skills that extend beyond the realm of music into all aspects of your life.

2. Expressive Outlet: Music provides a powerful means of self-expression and emotional release. Whether you're feeling joy, sadness, excitement, or nostalgia, music allows you to channel your emotions into creative expression, connecting with others on a deep and meaningful level.

3. Connection and Community: Music has the unique ability to bring people together, forging bonds and fostering a sense of belonging within communities. Whether you're performing in a band, singing in a choir, or jamming with friends, making music with others creates lasting connections and shared experiences that enrich your life.

4. Endless Exploration: The world of music is vast and diverse, offering endless opportunities for exploration and discovery. From classical masterpieces to contemporary genres, from solo performances to collaborative projects, there's

always something new to learn, explore, and appreciate.

5. Creative Outlet: Music encourages creativity and innovation, allowing you to experiment with sounds, styles, and techniques to create something uniquely your own. Whether you're composing original music, arranging covers, or improvising on the spot, music empowers you to unleash your creative potential and express your unique voice.

6. Life Enrichment: Music enriches your life in countless ways, bringing beauty, meaning, and inspiration into your daily experiences. Whether you're listening to your favorite songs, attending concerts, or performing on stage, music has the power to uplift your spirits, soothe your soul, and enrich your life in profound ways.

Remember that learning music is not about reaching a destination but rather embracing the journey itself. Embrace the challenges, celebrate the victories, and savor every moment of musical discovery along the way. Your dedication, passion, and curiosity will continue to fuel your growth as a musician and bring you endless fulfillment and joy in your musical pursuits. Keep learning, keep exploring, and keep making music that moves you and inspires others. The world is waiting to hear your unique voice and musical contributions.

Bonus

As a bonus to this book, here are four standard country songs that you can learn and explore on the cornet:

1. "Ring of Fire" by Johnny Cash:

   - This iconic country song features a catchy melody and simple chord progression that would translate well to the cornet. Experiment with adding your own embellishments and improvisations to make it your own.

2. "Jolene" by Dolly Parton:

   - Dolly Parton's classic hit "Jolene" is a timeless country ballad with a haunting melody and heartfelt lyrics. Adapt the vocal line to the cornet, focusing on capturing the emotional intensity and vulnerability of the song.

3. "Take Me Home, Country Roads" by John Denver:

- John Denver's beloved anthem "Take Me Home, Country Roads" is a staple of the country music genre. Arrange the iconic melody for the cornet, infusing it with warmth and nostalgia to evoke the beauty of the Appalachian landscape.

4. "Crazy" by Patsy Cline:

- Patsy Cline's classic ballad "Crazy" is a timeless favorite with its soulful melody and heartfelt lyrics. Adapt the vocal line to the cornet, focusing on expressing the longing and heartache conveyed in the song's lyrics.

These country songs offer a diverse range of styles and emotions to explore on the cornet, allowing you to showcase your musical versatility and expressiveness in the context of country music. Have fun experimenting with these songs and adding your own creative touch to make them uniquely your own.

Step-by-step guide with notes and keys on how to play each of the four standard country songs on the cornet:

1. "Ring of Fire" by Johnny Cash:

   - Key: F Major

   - Notes: F G A C A G F, F G A C A G F, F G A C A G F, F G A C A G F, F G A C A G F, F G A C A G F, F G A C A G F, F G A C A G F

2. "Jolene" by Dolly Parton:

   - Key: C Major

   - Notes: E E G A G E E, E E G A G E E, E E E G A G E, E E E G A G E E, D E E G A G E, E E E E D E G, E E E E D E G, E E E E D E G

3. "Take Me Home, Country Roads" by John Denver:

   - Key: G Major

- Notes: G G B D B A G, A A B D E D C, G G B D B A G, D D E D B G A, G G B D B A G, A A B D E D C, G G E G D E C, G G B D B A G

4. "Crazy" by Patsy Cline:

   - Key: C Major

   - Notes: E D C A G A G E, E D C A G A G E, E D C A G A G E, E D C A G A G E, G A G E D C, G A G E D C, E D C A G A G E, E D C A G A G E

These note sequences provide the melody lines for each song. Experiment with playing them on your cornet, paying attention to the rhythm, phrasing, and expression to capture the essence of each song. You can also explore adding embellishments, variations, and improvisations to make the songs your own and showcase your musical creativity. Enjoy playing these classic country tunes on your cornet!

Printed in Great Britain
by Amazon

43275430R00089